Contents

Welcome to "**Python Quickstart: The One Day, Easy Way Cookbook to Get You Cooking with Code**"! If you're looking for a comprehensive guide to getting started with Python programming, you've come to the right place. This book is designed for absolute beginners who have never coded before, as well as for experienced coders who want to pick up Python quickly.

The purpose of this book is to help you understand the basics of Python programming in one day. The lessons are designed to be easy to follow and include practical examples that help you apply the concepts you've learned. We'll start by covering the basics, such as variables, data types, and basic operations. Then, we'll dive into more advanced topics, such as functions, modules, and object-oriented programming.

By the end of this book, you'll have a solid foundation in Python programming and be able to write your own simple programs. You'll also have the knowledge and confidence to continue your journey as a Python programmer. So, let's get started and begin your journey towards becoming a skilled Python developer!

Setting up Your Python Development Environment

In this lesson, you will learn how to set up your computer for Python development. This includes installing the latest version of Python and a suitable code editor or integrated development environment (IDE).

Installing Python

The first step in setting up your Python development environment is to install the latest version of Python. You can download the latest version of Python from the official Python website (https://www.python.org/). After downloading, simply run the installer and follow the instructions to complete the installation process.

It is recommended to also install the latest version of pip, the package manager for Python, during the installation process. This will allow you to easily install and manage packages and libraries for your Python projects.

Choosing a Code Editor or IDE

The next step is to choose a code editor or IDE for writing and executing your Python code. There are many options to choose from, both free and paid. Some popular options include:

- Visual Studio Code (VSCode)

- PyCharm

- Sublime Text

- Atom

- IDLE (Python's built-in IDE)

It is important to choose a code editor or IDE that you feel comfortable with and provides the features and tools you need for your Python development.

Testing Your Python Installation

Once you have installed Python and a code editor or IDE, it is important to test your installation to ensure everything is set up correctly. You can do this by opening your code editor or IDE and creating a new file. In this file, enter the following code:

```python
print("Hello, World!")
```

Save the file with a .py extension (e.g. "hello_world.py"). Then, run the file to execute the code. If everything is set up correctly, you should see the output "Hello, World!" in the console or terminal window.

In this lesson, you have learned how to set up your computer for Python development by installing the latest version of Python and a suitable code editor or IDE. You have also tested your installation to ensure everything is set up correctly.

Understanding Variables, Data Types, and Basic Operations

In this lesson, you will learn about variables, data types, and basic operations in Python. Variables are used to store values, while data types determine the type of values that can be stored. Basic operations include arithmetic operations, comparisons, and logical operations.

Input Function

The **input()** function in Python allows you to receive input from the user in the form of a string. This string can then be used to perform various operations in your code. For example, you can ask the user for their name and store it in a variable like this:

```python
name = input("What's your name? ")
print("Hello, " + name + "!")
```

In this example, when you run the code, the program will prompt the user with the message "What's your name?" and wait for their response. The user's response will be stored in the name variable, and then used to print a personalized greeting. This allows you to make your programs more interactive and dynamic by allowing them to respond to input from the user

Print Function

The **print()** function in Python is used to display output to the console. It is one of the most commonly used functions for debugging and testing code. To use the **print()** function, simply pass the data that you want to display as an argument within the parentheses. For example:

```python
print("Hello, World!")
```

This code will display the string "Hello, World!" to the console. The **print()** function can be used to display a variety of data types, including strings, numbers, and even complex data structures such as lists and dictionaries.

Variables

Variables are used to store values in a program. In Python, you can create a variable by assigning a value to it using the assignment operator (=). For example:

```python
name = "John Doe"
age = 30
```

In this example, two variables name and age are created and assigned values. The variable name is assigned a string value, while the variable age is assigned an integer value.

Data Types

In Python, data types determine the type of values that can be stored in variables. Some of the most common data types in Python include:

- **int** (integer)
- **float** (floating-point number)
- **str** (string)
- **bool** (boolean)

You can determine the type of a variable using the built-in **type()** function:

```python
print(type(name))  # Output: <class 'str'>

print(type(age))   # Output: <class 'int'>
```

BTW, comments in Python are represented by the symbol "#". They are notes in the code that are ignored by the interpreter and provide explanations and annotations.

Basic Operations

Python supports a wide range of basic operations, including arithmetic operations, comparisons, and logical operations.

Arithmetic Operations

Arithmetic operations in Python include addition (+), subtraction (-), multiplication (*), division (/), and modulus (%). For example:

```
a = 10
b = 5
c = a + b   # Output: 15
d = a - b   # Output: 5
e = a * b   # Output: 50
f = a / b   # Output: 2.0
g = a % b   # Output: 0
```

In this example, variables a and b are assigned values, and various arithmetic operations are performed on these values.

Comparisons

Comparisons in Python include equal to (==), not equal to (!=), greater than (>), less than (<), greater than or equal to (>=), and less than or equal to (<=). For example:

```
a = 10
b = 5
print(a == b) # Output: False
print(a != b) # Output: True
print(a > b) # Output: True
print(a < b) # Output: False
print(a >= b) # Output: True
print(a <= b) # Output: False
```

In this example, variables a and b are assigned values, and various comparisons are performed on these values. The result of a comparison is a boolean value (True or False).

Logical Operations

Logical operations in Python include and (and), or (or), and not (not). For example:

```
a = True
b = False
print(a and b) # Output: False
print(a or b) # Output: True
print(not a) # Output: False
```

In this example, variables a and b are assigned boolean values, and various logical operations are performed on these values.

Keywords

In Python, keywords are reserved words that have special meanings and cannot be used as variable names or any other identifiers. There are 35 keywords in Python 3.

And	As	Assert	Async	Await	Break	Class
Continue	Def	Del	Elif	Else	Except	False
Finally	For	From	Global	If	Import	In
Is	Lambda	None	Nonlocal	Not	Or	Pass
Raise	Return	True	Try	While	With	Yield

As you progress through the chapters of this book, you will encounter various keywords in Python. It is important to not get discouraged if you are not familiar with their meanings at this moment. In the upcoming lessons, we will go over each keyword in detail and provide examples to help you understand their purpose and usage.

Example

```
# Take user input
num1 = float(input("Enter first number: "))

num2 = float(input("Enter second number: "))


# Perform operation
result = num1 + num2


# Print result
print("The sum of", num1, "and", num2, "is", result)
```

In this example, the program takes two numbers as input from the user, adds them together, and then prints the result. The **input()** function is used to get input from the user as a string, and the **float()** function is used to convert the string to a floating-point number. The result of the addition is stored in the result variable, and finally printed using the **print()** function.

In this lesson, you have learned about variables, data types, and basic operations in Python. Variables are used to store values, while data types determine the type of values that can be stored. Basic operations include arithmetic operations, comparisons, and logical operations. It's important to understand these concepts as they form the foundation for writing more complex programs in Python. In the next lesson, you will learn about Python's built-in data structures, such as lists, tuples, dictionaries, and sets. These data structures allow you to organize and manipulate data in a more efficient manner.

Understanding Control Flow with If-Else Statements

In this lesson, you will learn about control flow and how to use if-else statements in Python to control the flow of your program. Control flow refers to the order in which statements are executed in a program.

If-Else Statements

The most basic form of control flow in Python is the **if-else** statement. An **if-else** statement allows you to conditionally execute a block of code based on a certain condition. If the condition is met, the code in the if block is executed. If the condition is not met, the code in the else block is executed. Here is an example:

```python
age = 20
if age >= 18:
    print("You are an adult.")
else:
    print("You are a minor.")
```

In this example, the variable age is assigned a value of 20. The condition age >= 18 is evaluated, and if it is True, the code in the if block is executed, printing "You are an adult." to the screen. If the condition is False, the code in the else block is executed, printing "You are a minor." to the screen.

You can also chain multiple if-else statements to handle multiple conditions. Here is an example:

```python
age = 20
if age >= 18:
    print("You are an adult.")
elif age >= 13:
    print("You are a teenager.")
else:
    print("You are a child.")
```

In this example, the variable age is assigned a value of 20. The first condition age >= 18 is evaluated, and if it is True, the code in the first if block is executed, printing "You are an adult." to the screen. If the first condition is False, the next condition age >= 13 is evaluated. If this condition is True, the code in the elif block is executed, printing "You are a teenager." to the screen. If all conditions are False, the code in the else block is executed, printing "You are a child." to the screen.

Boolean Expressions

A boolean expression is an expression that evaluates to either True or False. In if-else statements, the condition is a boolean expression. Here are some examples of boolean expressions:

```
a = 5

b = 10

c = a == b

print(c) # Output: False


d = a < b

print(d) # Output: True


e = (a + b) > 15

print(e) # Output: False
```

In this example, variables a and b are assigned values. The expressions a == b, a < b,

And (a + b) > 15 are evaluated, and the results are stored in the variables c, d, and e

respectively. The variables c, d, and e now contain the boolean values False, True, and False

respectively.

Example

Here's an example of a simple program that uses if, elif, and else statements to determine

the grade of a student based on their percentage score:

```python
# input the percentage score
score = float(input("Enter the student's percentage score: "))


# determine the grade based on the score
if score >= 90:
    grade = "A"
elif score >= 80:
    grade = "B"
elif score >= 70:
    grade = "C"
elif score >= 60:
    grade = "D"
else:
    grade = "F"


# output the grade
print("The student's grade is:", grade)
```

In this example, the program first prompts the user to input a percentage score. The score is then used to determine the grade by evaluating different conditions in the if, elif, and else statements. Finally, the grade is printed to the screen.

Understanding Loops in Python

In this lesson, you will learn about loops in Python and how they can be used to repeat a block of code multiple times. Loops are an important concept in programming as they allow you to automate repetitive tasks, making your code more efficient and easier to maintain.

There are two main types of loops in Python: for loops and while loops.

For Loops

A for loop is used to iterate over a sequence, such as a list or a string, and execute a block of code for each item in the sequence. Here is an example:

```python
fruits = ["apple", "banana", "cherry"]
for fruit in fruits:
    print(fruit)
```

In this example, a list of fruits is defined. The for loop iterates over the list, and for each iteration, the value of the current item is assigned to the variable fruit. The code in the loop block is executed, and the value of fruit is printed to the screen. This process continues until all items in the list have been processed. The output of this code will be:

```
apple

banana

cherry
```

While Loops

A while loop is used to execute a block of code as long as a certain condition is true. Here is an example:

```
count = 0

while count < 5:

    print(count)

    count += 1
```

In this example, the variable count is assigned a value of 0. The while loop checks the condition count < 5 and if it is True, the code in the loop block is executed, printing the value of count to the screen. The value of count is then incremented by 1. The loop continues to repeat as long as the condition count < 5 is True. The output of this code will be:

```
0

1
```

The break and continue Statements

In loops, you can use the break statement to exit the loop prematurely, and the continue statement to skip the current iteration and move on to the next one. Here is an example using the break statement:

```
fruits = ["apple", "banana", "cherry"]
for fruit in fruits:
    if fruit == "banana":
        break
    print(fruit)
```

In this example, a list of fruits is defined. The for loop iterates over the list, and for each iteration, the value of the current item is assigned to the variable fruit. The code in the loop block checks if fruit is equal to "banana". If it is, the break statement is executed, and the loop is exited prematurely. The output of this code will be:

```
apple
```

Working with Lists, Tuples and Dictionaries

Lists

Lists are a powerful data structure in Python that allows you to store collections of items, whether they be of the same type or of different types. A list is defined using square brackets, and items are separated by commas. Here is an example of a simple list:

```python
fruits = ['apple', 'banana', 'cherry', 'orange']
```

In this example, we have created a list named fruits which contains four items: 'apple', 'banana', 'cherry', and 'orange'.

You can access individual items in a list using their index. The index of the first item in a list is 0, the second item is 1, and so on. Here is an example of accessing an item in a list:

```python
print(fruits[0])  # outputs: "apple"
print(fruits[2])  # outputs: "cherry"
```

There are several built-in functions you can use to manipulate lists. For example, you can use the **len()** function to get the number of items in a list:

```python
print(len(fruits))  # outputs: 4
```

You can use the **append()** function to add an item to the end of a list:

```
fruits.append("pear")

print(fruits)

# outputs: ["apple", "banana", "cherry", "orange", "pear"]
```

You can use the **insert()** function to insert an item at a specific position in a list:

```
fruits.insert(1, "grape")

print(fruits)

# outputs: ["apple", "grape", "banana", "cherry", "orange", "pear"]
```

You can use the **remove()** function to remove an item from a list:

```
fruits.remove("banana")

print(fruits)

# outputs: ["apple", "grape", "cherry", "orange", "pear"]
```

And you can use the **sort()** function to sort the items in a list:

```python
fruits.sort()

print(fruits)

# outputs: ["apple", "cherry", "grape", "orange", "pear"]
```

These are just a few examples of the built-in functions you can use with lists. In this lesson, you have learned the basics of working with lists in Python, including the syntax for creating a list, accessing items in a list, and using built-in functions to manipulate lists.

Tuples

A tuple is a data structure in Python that is similar to a list but with some important differences. A tuple is an immutable collection of elements, meaning that once a tuple is created, you can't change the elements in it. This makes tuples useful for representing data that should not be changed throughout the lifetime of a program.

A tuple is defined using round brackets () instead of square brackets [], which are used for lists. The elements in a tuple are separated by commas. Here's an example of how you can create a tuple in Python:

```
t = (1, 2, 3, 4)
print(t) # outputs (1, 2, 3, 4)
```

You can access the elements of a tuple using indexing, just like you would with a list. Here's an example:

```
print(t[0])  # outputs 1
print(t[2])  # outputs 3
```

One key difference between tuples and lists is that tuples are immutable, meaning you can't modify the elements once the tuple has been created. Lists are mutable, so you can add, remove, or modify elements in a list.

Despite their immutability, tuples have many of the same built-in functions as lists. For example, you can use the **len()** function to get the length of a tuple, and the **sorted()** function to sort the elements in a tuple.

```python
t = (4, 2, 3, 1)
print(len(t)) # outputs 4
print(sorted(t)) # outputs [1, 2, 3, 4]
```

Tuples are often used in Python to represent a collection of related values. For example, you might use a tuple to represent a point in a 2D space with x and y coordinates:

```python
point = (3,4)
x = point[0]
y = point[1]
print(x,y)

# outputs 3 4
```

In conclusion, tuples are a useful data structure in Python that offer a way to represent immutable collections of values. By using tuples, you can make sure that the values in your program won't change unexpectedly, which can make your code easier to understand and maintain.

Dictionaries

Dictionaries are one of the built-in data structures in Python, used to store key-value pairs. Unlike lists and tuples, which are ordered sequences, dictionaries are unordered collections. They allow you to store values by associating a unique key with each value. This allows you to access and retrieve values from the dictionary quickly and efficiently.

Defining Dictionaries:

Dictionaries are defined by enclosing a comma-separated list of key-value pairs within curly braces {}. The key-value pairs are separated by a colon (:). You can also use the **dict()** constructor to create dictionaries.

```
# Example 1: Defining a dictionary using curly braces

dict1 = {'key1': 'value1', 'key2': 'value2', 'key3': 'value3'}
print(dict1)



# Example 2: Defining a dictionary using the dict() constructor

dict2 = dict(key1='value1', key2='value2', key3='value3')
print(dict2)
```

Accessing Values:

You can access values in a dictionary by using the square brackets [] and providing the key. If the key is not present in the dictionary, a KeyError will be raised. You can use the **get()** method to retrieve the value of a key. The **get()** method returns None if the key is not present in the dictionary.

```
# Example: Accessing values in a dictionary

dict1 = {'key1': 'value1', 'key2': 'value2', 'key3': 'value3'}
print(dict1['key1'])
print(dict1.get('key4'))
```

Modifying Values:

You can modify the values of a dictionary by assigning a new value to the key. If the key is not present in the dictionary, a new key-value pair will be added.

```
# Example: Modifying values in a dictionary

dict1 = {'key1': 'value1', 'key2': 'value2', 'key3': 'value3'}
dict1['key1'] = 'new_value1'
print(dict1)
```

Removing Key-Value Pairs:

You can remove key-value pairs from a dictionary using the del keyword or the **pop()** method. The del keyword removes the key-value pair from the dictionary and the **pop()** method removes the key-value pair and returns the value.

```python
# Example: Removing key-value pairs from a dictionary

dict1 = {'key1': 'value1', 'key2': 'value2', 'key3': 'value3'}
del dict1['key1']
print(dict1)


value = dict1.pop('key2')
print(value)
print(dict1)
```

Dictionaries are a very useful data structure in Python, and they allow you to store and retrieve values efficiently. You can use them to store complex data structures or use them to efficiently count the occurrence of items in a list.

Functions

A function is a block of organized, reusable code that is used to perform a single, related action. Functions provide better modularity for your application and a high degree of code reusing. As your program grows larger and more complex, functions make it easy to break down tasks into smaller, manageable subtasks.

Defining a Function

In Python, a function is defined using the "def" keyword, followed by the function name, parentheses ( ), and a colon (:). The code inside the function should be indented, typically with 4 spaces.

```python
def function_name(arguments):
    # code here
    return [expression]
```

Function Arguments

Functions may or may not have arguments. Arguments are specified within the parentheses of a function, and are used to pass data into the function for processing. The syntax for function arguments is:

```
def function_name(arg1, arg2, arg3):
    # code here
    return [expression]
```

Returning a Value

The return statement is used to exit a function and return a value back to the caller. You can use any expression or data type as a return value.

```
def function_name(arg1, arg2, arg3):
    # code here
    return [expression]
```

Function Call

Once a function is defined, you can call it by using its name, followed by parentheses. You can also pass arguments into a function by putting them within the parentheses.

```
function_name(arg1, arg2, arg3)
```

Functions are a key building block in Python and a fundamental tool for breaking down complex problems into smaller, manageable parts. In the next lessons, we will dive into functions and their various use cases in greater detail.

Lambda Functions

Lambda functions, also known as anonymous functions, are small, single-line functions in Python that can be used to perform simple operations. Unlike regular functions, lambda functions don't have a name, and they can be written in one line of code. They are commonly used in situations where a short, throwaway function is required, such as in a filter or map function.

The syntax of a lambda function is as follows:

```
lambda arguments: expression
```

Here, the arguments are the inputs to the function, and the expression is the result that the function returns. The expression must always be a single statement, and the result of the expression is automatically returned.

Here's an example of a lambda function that takes two arguments and returns their sum:

```
sum = lambda x, y: x + y
print(sum(5, 10))
# Output: 15
```

In this example, we have defined a lambda function that takes two arguments, x and y, and returns their sum. The function is assigned to a variable, sum, and we can call it like any other function.

Lambda functions can also be used in combination with other functions such as map, filter, and reduce. For example, we can use a lambda function to double the values of a list:

```
numbers = [1, 2, 3, 4, 5]
doubled = list(map(lambda x: x*2, numbers))
print(doubled)
# Output: [2, 4, 6, 8, 10]
```

In this example, the map function takes two arguments: a lambda function and a list. The map function applies the lambda function to each item in the list, and returns a new list with the results.

In conclusion, lambda functions are a powerful tool in Python that can make your code more concise and readable. By using lambda functions, you can perform simple operations in a single line of code, and you can easily incorporate them into other functions such as map, filter, and reduce.

Variable scope

Variable scope in Python refers to the region of the program where a particular variable is defined and can be accessed. Understanding the scope of variables is important in writing efficient and effective code in Python. There are two types of variable scopes in Python: global and local.

Global Variables:

Global variables are defined outside of any function or class and can be accessed from anywhere in the program. They are also known as top-level variables, as they are not restricted to a particular function or class. Global variables are defined using the '**global**' keyword.

Example:

```python
x = 10 #global variable

def add_numbers():
    global x
    x = x + 5
    print("Inside the function, x =", x)

add_numbers()
print("Outside the function, x =", x)
```

Output:

```
Inside the function, x = 15
Outside the function, x = 15
```

Local Variables:

Local variables are defined inside a function or class and can only be accessed within that function or class. They are also known as function-level variables, as they are defined inside a function and are not accessible outside of it.

Example:

```python
def add_numbers():

    y = 5   #local variable

    x = 10


    print("Inside the function, x =", x)

add_numbers()
print("Outside the function, y =", y)
```

Output:

```
Inside the function, x = 10
NameError: name 'y' is not defined
```

In the example above, you can see that the variable y is not accessible outside of the function add_numbers, which makes it a local variable.

In conclusion, it is important to understand the scope of variables in Python, as it can affect the behavior and performance of your code. Always keep in mind the scope of your variables, and make sure that you are accessing them correctly.

Understanding Modules and Importing Packages

In this lesson, we will be discussing modules and packages in Python, and how they can be used to organize and structure your code. Modules and packages allow you to break down your code into smaller, reusable pieces, making it easier to maintain and test your code.

What is a Module in Python?

A module is a file containing Python definitions and statements. The file name is the module name with the suffix .py added. Modules can contain functions, classes, and variables, and can be imported into other modules to make use of their functionality.

How to import a Module in Python?

To import a module in Python, you use the import keyword. For example, to import the math module, you would write the following code:

```
import math
```

Once the module has been imported, you can access its functions, classes, and variables using the module name as a prefix. For example, to use the sqrt function from the math module, you would write the following code:

```
import math
print(math.sqrt(16))
```

What is a Package in Python?

A package is a collection of modules in a directory. The directory name is the package name. Packages can contain multiple modules and other packages, making it possible to organize your code into a hierarchical structure.

How to import a Package in Python?

To import a package in Python, you use the import keyword followed by the package name. For example, to import the numpy package, you would write the following code:

```
import numpy
```

Once the package has been imported, you can access its modules and other packages using the package name as a prefix. For example, to use the array module from the numpy package, you would write the following code:

```
import numpy
array = numpy.array([1, 2, 3, 4])
```

In conclusion, modules and packages are important tools for organizing and structuring your code in Python. By breaking down your code into smaller, reusable pieces, you can make your code easier to maintain and test, and you can also make use of existing code written by others.

Here are some of the most popular modules in Python:

NumPy: a library for numerical computing with support for arrays and matrices

Pandas: a library for data manipulation and analysis

Matplotlib: a library for data visualization

Seaborn: a library for data visualization based on Matplotlib

TensorFlow: a library for machine learning and deep learning

Pygame: a library for game development

Scikit-learn: a library for machine learning and data analysis

OpenCV: a library for computer vision

Pillow: a library for image processing

Requests: a library for making HTTP requests

These are just a few of the many modules available in Python. Each of these modules has a specific set of functions and classes that can be used to solve specific problems in your code.

Exception Handling in Python

Exception handling in Python is an important concept to understand when working with code. Exception handling allows you to handle errors and unexpected events in your program, making it more robust and reliable.

In Python, exceptions are raised when errors occur in your code. These errors can be due to various reasons, such as dividing by zero, accessing an index that does not exist, or opening a file that does not exist. When an exception occurs, the execution of your code stops and an exception is raised.

The built-in try and except statements in Python allow you to handle exceptions in your code. The try statement is used to enclose the code that may raise an exception. The except statement is used to handle the exception if one occurs. You can have multiple except statements to handle different types of exceptions.

For example:

```python
try:
    # code that may raise an exception
    result = 10 / 0
except ZeroDivisionError:
    print("Division by zero is not allowed.")
```

In this example, we are dividing 10 by 0, which is not allowed and raises a ZeroDivisionError exception. The except statement is used to handle this exception and print an error message.

You can also use the finally statement in combination with the try and except statements to execute code regardless of whether an exception occurs or not.

```
try:
    # code that may raise an exception
    result = 10 / 0
except ZeroDivisionError:
    print("Division by zero is not allowed.")
finally:
    print("This code will always run.")
```

In this example, the code inside the finally statement will always run, regardless of whether an exception occurs or not.

It's important to note that in Python, exceptions should be used for exceptional cases and not as a control flow mechanism. It's better to structure your code in a way that prevents exceptions from being raised in the first place, rather than relying on exception handling to fix problems after they occur.

File Input and Output in Python

In Python, file input and output (I/O) refers to the process of reading from and writing to files on your computer's storage. Python offers a number of ways to handle file I/O, ranging from simple to complex. In this lesson, we will cover the basics of reading from and writing to files in Python.

Reading from Files

To start reading from a file in Python, you first need to open the file using the built-in **open()** function. The **open()** function takes two arguments: the name of the file and the mode in which you want to open the file. The mode can be **'r'** for reading, **'w'** for writing, and **'a'** for appending to an existing file.

Here's an example of how to open a file and read its contents:

```
with open('example.txt', 'r') as file:
    contents = file.read()
    print(contents)
```

In this example, we use the with statement to open the file example.txt in read mode ('r'). The with statement ensures that the file is automatically closed after the indented block of code is executed. The **.read()** method is then used to read the contents of the file and store it in the contents variable. Finally, we print the contents of the file to the console.

Writing to Files

To write to a file in Python, you need to open the file in write mode ('**w**') or append mode ('**a**'). In write mode, any existing content in the file is overwritten, while in append mode, new content is added to the end of the file without overwriting existing content.

Here's an example of how to open a file in write mode and write to it:

```python
with open('example.txt', 'w') as file:
    file.write('Hello, World!')
```

In this example, we open the file example.txt in write mode ('**w**') using the with statement. We then use the **.write()** method to write the string 'Hello, World!' to the file.

That's it for the basics of reading from and writing to files in Python! There are many more advanced techniques for working with files in Python, such as reading and writing different file formats (e.g. CSV, JSON), reading and writing files in different encoding formats, and more. However, the concepts covered in this lesson should be enough to get you started with file I/O in Python.

An Introduction to Object-Oriented Programming in Python

Object-Oriented Programming (OOP) is a popular programming paradigm that is used in many modern programming languages, including Python. In this lesson, we will introduce the basic concepts of OOP and how to use them in Python.

1. Objects and Classes

In OOP, everything is represented as an object. An object is an instance of a class, which is a blueprint for creating objects. A class defines the properties and methods that an object can have. For example, we can define a class named "Car" that has properties such as "color", "make", "model", and "year".

2. Methods

Methods are functions that are associated with a class. They allow us to perform operations on the properties of an object. For example, we could have a method named "drive" that simulates driving a car. When we call the "drive" method on a car object, it changes the "speed" property of the car object.

3. Inheritance

Inheritance is a mechanism that allows us to create a new class based on an existing class. The new class inherits the properties and methods of the existing class and can add or override them. For example, we could create a class named "SportsCar" that inherits from the "Car" class and adds a "turbo" property.

4. Polymorphism

Polymorphism is the ability of an object to take on multiple forms. In OOP, polymorphism allows us to define methods in a base class that can be overridden by subclasses. This allows us to write code that can work with objects of different classes in a similar way.

5. Encapsulation

Encapsulation is the practice of hiding the implementation details of a class and only exposing the necessary information to the outside world. In Python, we can use the "private" and "protected" keywords to specify which methods and properties should be private or protected.

In conclusion, Object-Oriented Programming is a powerful programming paradigm that allows us to write clean, reusable, and maintainable code. In this lesson, we introduced the basic concepts of OOP, including objects, classes, methods, inheritance, polymorphism, and encapsulation. Understanding these concepts is essential for writing efficient and effective Python programs.

Congratulations on completing "**Python Quickstart: The One Day, Easy Way Cookbook to Get You Cooking with Code**"! By now, you should have a solid understanding of the basics of Python programming and be able to write your own simple programs.

Remember, the key to becoming a successful programmer is practice. So, keep practicing and experimenting with the concepts you've learned in this book. As you gain more experience, you'll start to develop your own style and approach to coding.

We hope this book has been helpful in starting your journey as a Python programmer. Remember, the sky is the limit! With hard work and dedication, the possibilities are endless. So, keep coding, keep learning, and never stop growing as a programmer.

Good luck and happy coding!

www.ingramcontent.com/pod-product-compliance
Lightning Source LLC
LaVergne TN
LVHW081806050326
832903LV00027B/2118